BALD EAGLE
VISION

JASON O'NEIL

authorHOUSE®

AuthorHouse™
1663 Liberty Drive
Bloomington, IN 47403
www.authorhouse.com
Phone: 1-800-839-8640

Published by AuthorHouse 5/24/2012

ISBN: 978-1-4772-0784-0 (e)
ISBN: 978-1-4772-0785-7 (sc)

Library of Congress Control Number: 2012908581

Any people depicted in stock imagery provided by Thinkstock are models, and such images are being used for illustrative purposes only. Certain stock imagery © Thinkstock.

This book is printed on acid-free paper.

Because of the dynamic nature of the Internet, any web addresses or links contained in this book may have changed since publication and may no longer be valid. The views expressed in this work are solely those of the author and do not necessarily reflect the views of the publisher, and the publisher hereby disclaims any responsibility for them.

TABLE OF CONTENTS

Chapter One:

"TAKING OFF"

"Erin, are you ready?"

"Yes."

"OK. Let's go."

My daughter and I boarded a seaplane in Anchorage, Alaska, for the 45-minute flight to the westernmost shore, a seaport called Homer. As we zoomed over the 50-foot conifer pines, I checked my camera equipment. I was particularly excited about this five-day "retreat" because I knew I was going to come face-to-face with America's national bird, the bald eagle. But the trip had a bigger meaning, which I was about to divulge to Erin. The eagle symbolized the real meaning of the voyage: How to save our republic.

As the plane skimmed across ice-blue rivers flanked by never-ending forests, I kept asking myself, "Why me? Why was I chosen for this mission? Will I succeed? What will be Erin's reaction to being chosen as the harbinger, indeed, the Paul Revere of the 21st century, to commence a revolution against the welfare state?"

This will be my best chance, over these next five days, and I dare not let the nation down, I thought. In many ways this was tougher than being a Marine officer in Vietnam. There, I fired shots on behalf of America's democratization of the planet. Now I must use analogies and carefully selected words to save our democracy from itself.

From the airplane we could see bears running from the prop noise, puffins on cliffs, and flocks of seagulls circling about schools of fish. I thought of "Jonathan Livingston Seagull," Richard Bach's simple explanation of individual freedom told through the story of one bird learning how to fly against the order of the flock. For me the flock symbolized a bureaucracy that squashed freedom and made the innovator an outcast.

The analogy to modern America – some 40 years later – is inescapable. America needs to pioneer flight once again. It will spur the national commitment to solving its debt crisis brought upon the nation in 1964 by Lyndon Johnson's Great Society. As young lads, my brother and I snuck into the nominating convention with phony press passes that year. I was too young to know the damage the Great Society would cause to our democracy. Everybody was. It was a political ploy to gain votes at the expense of the national treasury.

Now, I suddenly feel pressure to adequately explain the impact of the welfare state upon my daughter. Somehow she must be the patriot in the church tower who waves the lantern to alert his generation of the dangers that have infested the Great American Experiment in time to save our democracy.

As the seaplane gently floated to its pier at Homer Spit, I could hear somebody on the pier call out, "Welcome to Eagle Country! Here you will see many reasons why America is great."

As we took the water taxi south across the bay to the lodge, I kept thinking that America is an experiment. Our Revolution was unique inasmuch as the rebels won. A government by and for the people was established by a Constitution that was so well devised that only 26 amendments have been required in 226 years. When asked by a curious citizen after the adjournment of the Constitutional Convention what kind of government had been created by the Founding Fathers, Ben Franklin is said to have replied, "A republic, if you can keep it." Franklin must have known just what an ambitious undertaking the new America was.

It's been 2000 years since the Greeks flourished. What makes Americans think they can succeed? In some measure it's the pioneer spirit, like the Alaskan Gold Rush, that says the republic can solve society's biggest problems. Somehow I will have to explain this to my daughter in a way that makes "common cents." In other words, she must clearly understand the urgency of solution for our national debt, or her generation – those age 25 through 50 – will be relegated to a meager, perhaps subsistent

3

lifestyle, with no hope of retirement. The bald eagle will have to fly above the millions of ordinary citizens called to revolt against the establishment in Washington for this Great American Experiment to continue.

As the sun set behind a 13,000-foot mountain range, the water taxi pulled up to the lodge's pier. I thought to myself, this is when my salesmanship skills must shine. My logic must persuade and ultimately be employed by millions of patriots. It's a challenge that must be taken.

"Erin, let's check in and then join the other guests around the campfire."

Within a half-hour we were enjoying venison stew and homemade biscuits while warming ourselves with imported spirits alongside a blazing fire. Embers streamed up into the night sky, becoming one with the millions of stars twinkling in the cold, clear Alaskan night.

Soon, Erin's curiosity got the best of her. "Dad, what's our plan for the next five days? What are we going to do and why?"

"Well, Erin, it's simple. I thought we would have some meaningful conversations while enjoying the great outdoors. We'll fish, hike, canoe and kayak while I practice my photography, and hopefully we'll see some bald eagles. How does that sound?"

"It sounds like great fun. But there's got to be more."

"What do you mean?"

"Well, like your father and his father, you're a teacher. You don't drag me all the way up here just to commune with nature. Let's face it. You don't have the patience for fishing. Besides, I remember you telling me that when you were a teenager, you came here and the mosquitoes and horseflies were so bad, you couldn't get back in the airplane fast enough!"

"You're right, but this time I'm a man on a mission: I'm determined to take some great pictures and looking forward to enjoying this time together outdoors."

"And ..."

"And share with you some thoughts about our republic, our democracy and the current state of affairs." As we stared into the fire, I thought to myself that, in a perfect world, this father-daughter chat should take place a million times around America.

"Remember, Dad, I'm a journalist seasoned in asking tough questions."

"Yes you are. I know you'll question my facts and logic, and I'm looking forward to it."

"I have to admit, I am, too."

The fire glowed, but the long day had taken its toll on me. "What do you say we hit the hay and start early tomorrow?"

"Fine with me. The fish feed early."

The next morning came too soon. Dressed in our new fishing vests and several layers of clothing, we washed down a few hot cinnamon rolls with black coffee and were escorted to the pier by the innkeeper. He had already prepared our boat for the expedition, complete with paddles, rods, a bait box, lunch box and an environmentally friendly five-horsepower motor. Together we checked our map.

"Just hug the shore and you'll be fine," the innkeeper said. "There's a cove about a mile east. You'll know it when you get there – there are a lot of unsuccessful casts hanging from the tree limbs! But it's sheltered from the wind and full of salmon this time of year. If you see an eagle, take a picture. If you see a bear, stay in the boat. And be sure to return by 4 or you'll have to fight the tide. The motor's up to it, but only barely. Oh, and here's your mosquito lotion – get used to the smell. Good luck!"

"Thanks, we'll need it!"

Erin started the motor while I tied everything down and clutched my Nikon to my chest. We quickly got our sea legs and putt-putted along the shore toward the warming sunrise. Before long we found the cove and anchored. I said a silent prayer that my expensive fly-fishing lessons would pay off with a prize for dinner.

Wildlife was everywhere. I swear we saw each of Alaska's 493 bird species in the cove. I took pictures between fly casts. An hour passed.

"Dad, I got one!" Erin yelled. With the rod bending under the strain, it took us 10 minutes to net our first catch – a beauty – a rainbow trout that weighed in at about 6 pounds. I snapped a picture of the happy angler with her prize.

My rod, however, saw no action. Maybe it was due to my amateur skills, or perhaps my Irish luck had deserted me. Whatever the reason, there was a lull, so I decided to start my lesson.

"Erin, have you ever heard of the French nobleman, Alexis de Tocqueville?"

"No. Why?"

"Because he had some real insights into our young nation's character. He toured America in the 1830s and reported to his fellow Frenchmen the accomplishments of the 'Great American Experiment,' a phrase he borrowed from George Washington."

I pulled out a small piece of paper from my vest pocket and read from the introduction to De Tocqueville's classic, "Democracy in America," written by the Honorable John T. Morgan: "… the principles established in the Constitution and the check upon hasty or inconsiderate legislation, and upon executive action, and the supreme arbitrament of the courts, will be found sufficient for the safety of personal rights."

I moved on to the Frenchman's observations. "In Chapter IV, de Tocqueville writes of the United States, 'there society governs itself for itself.' In the following chapter he states, 'the principle of the sovereignty of the people governs the whole political system.' And finally, in Chapter IX he concludes, 'The people is therefore the real directing power. … In the United States the majority governs in the name of the people … and (is) sincerely desirous of the welfare of their country.'"

Erin seemed captivated, so I continued.

"For over two centuries Americans have kept the republic strong even though the advance of individual freedom and democracy has not been easy. We've overcome economic depressions and won world wars. Americans truly believe 'that all men are created equal, that they are endowed by their Creator with certain unalienable rights, that among these are life, liberty and the pursuit of happiness.' It is the moral foundation of their experiment. But guess what."

"What?

"This Great American Experiment is now at the crossroads of its very existence."

"What do you mean? We're not in a depression, at least not yet, and we're not under siege by some foreign power. And we patent more new inventions than the rest of the world."

"That's true. But we're suffering from three diseases that, if left unchecked, will destroy our republic and way of life."

"Three diseases at the same time?"

"Unfortunately, yes. And they are interrelated and genuine threats in our society."

"What are they?"

"Work ethic, bureaucracy and debt."

"Those are very important topics, Dad. But why did we have to travel 5,000 miles to this wilderness to discuss them?"

"Because there's no better place on earth. We're in a state that's home to 50,000 bald eagles, the very symbol of our republic. And there's no flat-screen TV in our cabin, no bars on the cell phone. Oh, and don't forget that fine fish you just caught!"

"Fine, we're isolated. But you've got a lot of explaining to do. Please hand me a beer, and I'll try not to let my liberal philosophies divert me from listening to your logic."

"OK. That's all I ask. Indeed, the topics are so important, I don't think we should rush through them. I thought I'd address one a day until the solution becomes evident at the end of the week."

"OK with me. But I still want to commune with nature. And I feel it's only fair to warn you that I'm a bit skeptical."

"I understand. I only ask that you allow me to explain my logic and listen with an open mind – that's something that's in very short supply these days. Let's tie up the boat and have a bite to eat. I think I'll even indulge in a beer with lunch; even the beer tastes better up here."

As we settled in with our sandwiches, I began to state my case.

"So let me start with a very simple thesis: The heart of both democracy and capitalism is individual freedom. Government bureaucracies can control and even prohibit this freedom. Indeed, 'Big Government' is convinced it can manage individuals better than if they are left to their own devices. This in turn diminishes the very work ethic that made this country so prosperous. Today, the federal government controls one-sixth of the economy. It employs millions of people. Unfortunately, the system and the majority of the civil servants have a work ethic that does not promote or reward efficiencies. And, worse yet, the civil servant is trapped, perhaps seduced by a 'you owe it to me' attitude toward the private citizens they are paid to serve."

"So, what does all this mean?"

"It means that the lack of work ethic (disease number one) leads to and is fostered by the bureaucratic welfare state (disease number two), resulting in an unsustainable debt (disease number three) – all feeding on the body republic at the same time. In other words, there is a vicious cycle which must be broken to ensure the survival of individual freedoms. It's time for a national radiation treatment."

"That's a good metaphor, Dad."

"Thanks. I think it works well in this scenario. To put it simply, the deteriorated work ethic – I don't have to work hard because the state will provide it for me – is so attractive that individuals flee to the bureaucracy – federal, state and local – for life security. Then their job is to keep their job at the expense of the delivery of efficient services that foster a free-enterprise economy. The welfare state exists for the welfare of the bureaucrats who rob the rights of individuals and replace them with laws and programs that do not create jobs in the private sector. This ensures tyranny by the minority, which was not the intention of our Founding Fathers."

"Does my logic hold up so far?"

"I guess so. But tell me more about this vicious cycle that you mentioned."

"It's pretty straightforward. The Nanny State's work ethic leads to a growth in the Government bureaucracy which, by its nature, must increase the national debt on behalf of "Joe" American. However, the bureaucracy only succeeds in growing itself and not increasing private sector jobs. Joe remains out of work, exhausts his savings, and, therefore, loses freedoms like moving to where people are hiring, staying healthy, retiring and enjoying the personal fulfillment of creating a product or service as a contributor in our economy. On a national scale this means the Good old USA can't create globally competitive goods and services. And this vicious cycle further impacts our free-enterprise system with an increased number of citizens flocking to the shelter of the Welfare Nanny. "

"See, Erin, the bureaucracy of the welfare state lowers society's work ethic while creating and passing on debilitating debt. And, as politicians have learned, you don't make people happier by taking their options away. As a result, they promise more handouts to continue a cycle that crushes individual freedoms.

"If I were to draw a picture in the sand of this riverbank, there would be three overlapping circles creating a small triangle in the middle. The circles would represent the reduced Work Ethic, Welfare State and National Debt. In the center would be a stick figure of the American

Citizen being invaded by these three diseases. One disease is tough enough to fight. However, when three attack the citizen simultaneously, well, it's a crisis with no historical precedent."

"That's a pretty scary situation, Dad."

"And national leaders don't know how to solve the problem. Not because they're stupid. They simply live in a fantasy world and want to protect their income and status by passing the problem to the next generation as they have for the past 50 years. In my opinion, time has run out. Your generation must solve the crisis my generation created and fostered."

"Why my generation?"

"Let me put it in perspective. On January 1, 1791, the national debt was $75 million. Today, our country's debt rises by that amount every hour! It's a formula for creating a Third World country where hard-working citizens will never be able to retire. Think about it. The state of Alaska – all 586,000 square miles of it – was purchased in 1867 for $7.2 million, or one-tenth of this hourly increase!"

"So, you're saying it's time to act before things get any worse."

"Exactly. And speaking of time, the sun's going down and it's almost 4. What do you say we head back to the lodge? Your one fish makes for a successful day. Maybe we'll see a bald eagle tomorrow."

Chapter Two:
"WORK ETHIC"

"Ready to hit the trail, Erin?"

"Yep. That lumberjack breakfast should keep me going on the hike."

"Agreed. The innkeeper says we should be fine if we stick to the trail. It's well marked with signs pointing back here, just in case. And evidently there's an eagle's nest at the turnaround point."

Walking sticks in hand, we set out toward the sunrise. Fifteen minutes into the hike, I called to Erin to come look at a trillium flower. The light purple blossom was illuminated by a single ray of light breaking through the pines.

"I need to take a picture – this is an endangered species in the Lower 48! What a rare treat, and something tells me there will be others throughout the day."

After an hour's forced march to keep up with Erin, I needed a rest. "Let's take a break on these rocks," I suggested.

"Sounds good. You know, I'm not as young as I used to be."

"You? What about me? I haven't kept up this pace since the Marine Corps."

The time and setting seemed an ideal opportunity to introduce my first topic.

"How about something to think about during the next leg?"

"OK, Dad, I'll bite. What's the issue this time?"

"Today's topic is one of the leading contributors to our nation's economic problems. It's something that affects you every day, but you can't do anything about it."

"Let me guess. Drug abuse or alcoholism?"

"No. Good guesses, but what's ailing America is much worse. It's everywhere in society – all states, classes and races – and it's the most difficult problem to remedy. It's the deterioration of the work ethic."

"OK. I'm all ears, but I'm also eager to keep hiking."

"I understand. I'll be brief."

We stretched out on the rocks and gazed out over a babbling brook nearby.

"First, we need a quick look back in history. Work ethic deterioration, indeed collapse, befell both ancient Greece and Rome. In 'The History of the Decline and Fall of the Roman Empire,' historian Edward Gibbons explained why Rome succumbed to the Goths in A.D. 410. There were many reasons – the rise of the Catholic Church and Islam, which challenged the emperor's power; debased currency; rampant inflation; the overextension of the empire to foreign lands that could not be managed; and, finally, the decadence of the citizenry. The middle and upper classes frowned upon work, instead preferring to 'lounge and lead.' In the end, a poorly trained military was no match for the Goths."

"Wait a minute, Dad. They had inflation in those days?"

"Sure they did. You see, the government kept minting more coins to pay for silks and spices. And when the Barbarians looted the treasury, the empire crumbled and medieval history began around A.D. 476."

"Are you saying this is an analog of what's happening today in America?"

"Absolutely!"

"You see, the problem is, in a word, debt. Debt is created by the welfare state, which can't function efficiently because of the lost work ethic. In the classic sense, 'work' is defined as the movement of a weight over a distance – like when the slaves moved rocks to build the pyramids. But moving a pile of paper from the in-basket to the out-basket without adding value – like building wealth in the economy – is not the 'work' that will solve the nation's problems."

"And you're going to wait until Friday to tell me what the solution is?"

"Yes. You need to understand my logic before you can appreciate, and perhaps even support, the solution."

I pointed to a nearby fern. "Erin, look at that."

"What? I only see a fern."

"Look closely!"

"Oh, I see it now. It's a bird – a *big* bird."

"It's a willow ptarmigan, the Alaskan state bird. It's a hearty species that's graceful in flight and fiercely protective of its young. "

"Dad, let's get moving."

"OK, but let's slow down a bit. We need to absorb this glorious setting, and if you don't gallop out in front of me, I can build the work ethic case along the path."

Not far down the path we stopped at the edge of a clearing to soak in the thousand shades of green. I then began to detail my observations about the causes of America's poor work ethic.

"Erin, for argument's sake, I lump the causes of this phenomenon into four categories: private sector, public sector, the public education system and the personal, or household, category.

"First let's talk about the private sector. In a global economy, businesses must produce a good or service while competing with companies from parts of the world where there are lower wage scales or superior products. This forces companies to cut midlevel positions. I know this firsthand: I was fired four times during my sales career. The companies also close factories and outsource jobs to foreign countries. Car engines, for example, are made in dozens of countries. This marks the depersonalization of manufacturing, because the employee who's left doesn't see the finished product, much less the customer. As a result, unions and trade organizations have great difficulty inspiring 'work excellence' and decent conditions, and most find themselves outdated.

"In short, corporate survival trumps customer service. As for the few who start their own company, they're usually the ones who can't find work or think they have a better mousetrap. Sadly, next to restaurants, start-ups have the highest fatality rate in the economy. The self-starter succumbs to the 80-hour work week, throws up his hands and seeks new employment, usually in a 'burned-out' state of mind."

"I get the picture. So then what happens?"

"They turn to a 'secure' work environment: the federal and state governments."

"Wait a minute. Not everybody does."

"True. But across America there are millions of people employed by federal, state and local governments. Many see it as an escape from the private sector, a place where they can get both job security and increased benefits, often at a higher salary and frequently while working at a relaxed work pace."

"And don't tell me. The welfare state grows."

"Yes, exactly. And this leads me to the second category of lower work ethic in this pretty land of ours: the public sector welfare state infrastructure."

"Sounds interesting. Go on."

"Have you been to Washington, D.C., lately? It's full of hundreds of buildings, including many new ones, full of hundreds of thousands of employees who exploit the system for personal benefit. They do not create goods and services that compete in the global economy – you can't process Social Security forms in Thailand, after all – so there's no competition or potential outsourcing in that regard. It's no wonder that four out of the top five wealthiest counties in America surround Washington, D.C.

"It's pretty simple, Erin. Even the most well-meaning intern gets seduced by the system of self-promotion and benefit creep. Do you realize that a bureaucratic couple in their twenties working the system for 30 years can receive six retirement checks every month when they are 60 years old – all at taxpayer expanse – for another 30 to 40 years? It's unsustainable. But this is only the tip of the iceberg. To make matters worse, our welfare state policy-makers create programs in the name of the unemployed or subsistence households that dole out billions in government checks, thus increasing the debt.

"Today I'm fearful I won't have enough money for retirement. I can only imagine how you feel. This damaging cycle must come to an end – and soon. If the hard-working people of Keokuk, Iowa – or Homer, Alaska, for that matter – knew what is really happening in Washington, they would revolt.

"Dad, you're ruining my appetite, but let's stop for lunch at the edge of that lake anyway."

"Sounds good. But keep in mind I haven't even mentioned the two fundamental sectors in our society that literally drive people to require the welfare state: the education system and the personal work ethic."

And with that we dove into the sandwiches our innkeeper had prepared for us. As we stood to continue, I stretched and turned to warm my face in the sun. Suddenly, something caught my eye.

"Erin, do you see what I see? It's the eagle nest!"

"Wow, it looks huge! And it's probably at least 60 feet off the ground!"

"Let's move over there, where I can set up my tripod and have a blue sky backdrop."

We packed up the last of our lunch and started toward the spot I had indicated.

"You know, in essence, this trip is all about the eagle – the bald eagle," I said.

"How so?"

"Well, while you're looking through the binoculars, I'll tell you some things about the bald eagle. Did you know that they died off so quickly in the 1960s that they were labeled an endangered species? Sport hunters and 'bounty' protectors of the fishing grounds killed thousands. But the real killer was pesticide. Eagles mainly eat fish, and pesticides collect in the fish. These chemicals weaken the birds' eggshells and thus severely limit their ability to reproduce. But in 1972 the use of DDT pesticide was outlawed, and today there are over 50,000 bald eagles in Alaska, and they can be found across America. It's an amazing success story."

"Dad, look!"

"Oh … my … God!"

There, right above us, maybe 100 feet up, was a bald eagle preparing to land on the nest.

"What a magnificent creature. No wonder he's at the top of the food chain."

I aimed my telephoto lens at this regal raptor, admiring its 7-foot wingspan as I shot frame after frame. We quickly understood why the eagle is the national bird of America, with its likeness on the currency, stamps and even the presidential seal.

"Erin, did you know that it takes five years before a bald eagle has a white head?"

"Dad, is this part of your font of useless knowledge?"

"I guess so – there's a lot more where that came from!"

After the eagle dropped its prey into the nest, it perched up on the edge and surveyed the landscape.

I aimed my camera … and couldn't believe what I saw.

"Erin, that bird only has one leg!"

"What do you mean it only has one leg?"

"Here. Look for yourself."

"Oh my gosh, you're right."

"He must have lost it in a hunter's trap. You know, only 50 percent of bald eagles survive to age 5."

"Imagine doing it with only one leg. It's tough enough to snatch salmon from the water with two talons. And he must be successful – he has a family to raise."

A trillium, a willow ptarmigan and now a bald eagle. I knew today would be really special, but I couldn't foresee this.

"Look, he's about to take off!"

In an instant, his spread-eagle wings were supporting his body as he glided down toward the lake.

"What do you think, Erin? I think this alone has made the trip worthwhile. Look at these pictures. I'm no professional, but I'm going to frame some of them."

As the proud raptor disappeared over the tree line, we packed our gear and headed back down the trail.

"You know, I'm glad that eagle doesn't know what trouble our nation faces," I said.

"Yeah, and I bet you're going to say that much of it stems from a weak public education system."

"You know me too well. But let me tell you, when I was a student in the 1950s and 1960s, we ran to the school bus. We were in good physical shape and had to be ready to endure a long Cold War. Today, the students waddle to the bus, take their seat and immediately disappear into the la la land of a cell phone or iPod."

"To make matters worse, the federal welfare state bureaucrats have forced a 'No Child Left Behind' program into every school district. It's a dismal attempt to equalize social classes through the school system under the guise of standardized student 'achievement.' It forced parents who were really interested in their child's education to enroll them in expensive private schools. During the program test scores went down and a quiet class struggle emerged. It's flawed, Erin, because the notion of everybody MUST succeed will never replace the RIGHT to do so. The standards quickly deteriorate, no matter how good a teacher may be, while students advance regardless of substandard performance. Where these lowered expectations are really obvious is in the concept of 'The Right to Do Over.'"

"What's 'The Right to Do Over'?"

"It has become common in our schools for students to ask to retake tests or rewrite papers in order to get a better grade. Usually the students who make this request are not failing. They want to push their grade from a B to an A to artificially inflate their GPA. If they are given the chance, they may not succeed, but you can bet the student expects a better grade merely for the effort."

"As an article in The New York Times recently put it: 'Such students see grades as pay for time spent on the job, not the quality of the product.' It's no wonder a 'clock punching' attitude toward schoolwork — and ultimately real-world employment — emerges."

"And, finally, you're aware of "grade inflation" at many universities. This gives a misleading picture of how the student's work stacks up against others'. They lack realistic feedback to improve, and then they get a real shock when their first boss in the private sector expects better performance. And, as often is the case, continued mediocre performance leads to declining self-esteem and a further deterioration of the work ethic. Everybody loses: the employee, the employer and the national economy.

"It's no wonder that the U.S. ranks 26th in the quality of education and that the public sector is so attractive. But we *are* first in something. In his 2010 documentary, 'Waiting for Superman,' filmmaker Davis Guggenheim revealed that, while the United States ranks below many other nations in the quality of the education it provides its children, our students rank first in confidence. It seems all that self-esteem building by passing students along and inflating grades has given our youth an unrealistic view of their own capabilities."

"Dad, I think you're right about a lot of these things. But let's face it. This has been like a sermon in the forest. Let's take a break from analyzing our nation's problems until we're at the bonfire at the lodge."

"Sounds like a plan. I'll bring the marshmallows." We hiked the last half-mile in silence.

After a dinner that would have fed a lumberjack *and* his family, the guests at the lodge gathered around the bonfire. Some sang songs. Others told fishing tales. I reflected upon the majestic eagle while adroitly toasting my marshmallow to perfection.

Suddenly Erin broke the silence. "Dad, I'm sorry I shut you down on that work ethic business. But it's pretty depressing, you know – about not being able to retire ... ever. And I just wasn't ready to hear you address the real crux of the matter – the disappearing personal work ethic in the good ol' USA."

"Thanks, but no apology is necessary. You're right on both counts. It's depressing. And I was about to deliver a sermon on the worst aspect of our nation's problem: the personal work ethic. It's not completely gone, but like the bald eagle, we're ingesting a pesticide that can kill our future.

"If you have a couple minutes I can summarize my observations."

"Sure. I'm not leaving the fire – I'm warm on one side and cold on the other."

"Well, here goes. There are a lot of factors that influence a person's work ethic. The main one is not genetic; it's environmental."

"First, you have to admit you grew up in a pretty pampered generation. You never had to survive a depression or march off to war. You and most of your peers had a car, a summer job, your own bedroom. In short, you didn't have to work, just enjoy life until after school, when reality appeared.

"Second, your generation became addicted to leisure time. You take every holiday plus a month's vacation. You and your friends are offended when work invades your private time. And if you have to work overtime, you try, sometimes with success, to extract a 'pound of flesh' from your boss.

"Third, because you see what's happening to the economy, your generation rationalizes that there is no need to save money. Hence, you live for today and assume that somehow the welfare state will take care of you four decades into the future.

"Fourth, in today's economy, with one out of six people either out of work, working part time or no longer looking for work, your parents are losing to the global economy and passing the burned-out torch to you. You wake up asking, 'Why should I bust my fanny today?'

"Fifth, because of the prolonged unemployment, either personally or in the family, society becomes addicted to welfare one person at a time."

"Sixth, to add to the problem, the nation's taxation policy is bankrupt. The federal government takes too much of a person's salary to pay for social programs the bureaucrats think we need. So why work any harder? The government will only assess a penalty for being in a higher tax bracket."

"Seventh, and now I'm running out of fingers, we're witnessing the rise of the social media. With trillions of text messages, your generation goes electronic to pass the hurt of personal isolation."

"I'm convinced that this is why so many members of the current generation can't look up from a crystal display and look somebody in the eye. And guess what?"

"What?"

"The first rule of a job interview is to look your potential employer in the eye."

"Right."

"And of course all of the above traits run counter to what the French theologian, John Calvin, was teaching two centuries ago. Calvin preached that those people chosen by God would enjoy eternal life. And in order to achieve eternal life, Calvin said, all men (and women) must work, even the rich, because to work is the will of God and a means for Eternal Rewards . Other religions preach the same thing. The point is simple: Fear and the pursuit of success push a lot of people through the factory gate."

"I hope it's clear that the loss of work ethic is one of the primary contributors to America's current situation. Our society could take a lesson from the bald eagle. Imagine how much work went into that 8-foot nest … and with only one leg."

Chapter Three:
"THE FLOCK"

"Erin, my arms feel like lead. I'm too old to be paddling a canoe all day! But it was fun seeing the fish in the crystal clear water. I'm sure I got some great pictures, too. It's neat when the blue water blends into the blue sky, framing snow-capped mountains."

"I agree. And seagulls – how about those flocks of seagulls? They're very powerful fliers, and boy are they sneaky. They'll find a meal almost anywhere!"

"I think I got some good pictures of them, too. Now let's take advantage of these rocking chairs and enjoy a drink as we talk about another subject. It's another type of flock: the human bureaucracy."

"The second disease in our body republic is the welfare state. The government bureaucracy exists to engineer society into equality. It does so by creating an unsustainable bureaucracy that submerges the work ethic while creating debts that, if unpaid, are capable of destroying our republic."

"Dad, I'm getting used to these dialogs. Let me guess. The bald eagle doesn't need to fly in a flock. It survives in a solitary role on top of the food chain."

"You nailed that one, my daughter."

"And let me guess again. There are questions about the current welfare state that need answers."

"Right again! There are three of them: How did the federal government build the current welfare state? How does the welfare state squash individual freedoms – both within the 'flock' and throughout society? And how do we limit the welfare state in order to eliminate the national debt?"

I sipped on my Canadian whiskey and answered the first question.

"Ever heard of the Great Society? In 1964, President Lyndon Johnson created many federal initiatives to bring Americans out of poverty, eliminate illiteracy and reduce pollution. This was the start of the welfare government 'whiz kids' who thought they knew what was best for the free individual. Thus a new 'nanny state' was born. Today, nearly 50 years later, this onslaught of entitlement programs is bankrupting America and suppressing individual freedoms for which our liberal founders broke away from the monarchy."

"Scottish jurist and historian Sir Alexander Fraser Tyler is often credited with saying, 'A democracy cannot exist as a permanent form of government. It can only exist until the voters discover they can vote themselves largesse from the public treasury. From that moment on, the majority always votes for the candidates promising the most benefits from the pubic treasury.'

"Odds are, LBJ didn't know Sir Tyler existed. He was simply buying votes under the guise of creating a war on poverty administered by bureaucrats in Washington. But the nation was seduced by a welfare mentality that believed government payments were as legitimate as bank checks in the private sector."

"Of all those who fell victim to the welfare mentality, none suffered more than the black communities. As a blogger who calls himself StoneGiant lamented in September 2005, 'Compare (the 1960s) to the present state of the black community after 40 years of Liberal Socialism. Our prisons are (disproportionately) black, unwed mothers and single parent families are the rule, black youths without a strong male role model other than rap stars and basketball players roam the streets and are drawn into a culture of drugs and crime.'

"It's become so bad that women have children in order to receive more money from the government. And they don't want to get married because a relationship with a boyfriend does not jeopardize their government check."

"The Great Society created food stamps, rent subsidies, Medicare, Medicaid and whole bureaucratic entities like the Department of Housing and Urban Development. As a result, as author Richard M. Ebeling said in a 2011 lecture, 'an underclass of more or less permanent wards of the state was created with intergenerational dependency on government transfers growing in frequency.'

"It's easy to see why much of the current budgetary and related debt crisis has its origin in LBJ's Great Society. It's even more profound when you realize that LBJ was fighting a war in Vietnam at the same time. Sound familiar?"

"Yup."

"In effect, Erin, it's really a tragedy of unintended consequences. The family unit breaks down and entitlement mentality becomes a social cancer. Let me put it in perspective. In 1965, under LBJ, the Feds spent 30.9 percent of the budget on human resources, aka 'social welfare programs.' In 1985 under President Reagan, the Feds spent 49.9 percent on human resources. In 2005, the Feds spent about 64 percent. In 2011 it approached 70 percent.

"See what's happening? Government's controls, regulations, redistribution of income efforts and just plain handouts are the exact opposite of what is needed in a free-enterprise system. Only the bureaucrats in Washington, D.C., and at state capitals win while we sink deeper in debt. And the individual's work ethic is a fatality of the entitlement mentality, too. It's a trap."

"Indeed, the Federal Reserve has but one action – monetize the debt by printing more money just to pay the interest on the debt. As Mr. Ebeling puts it, '... (the) welfare state agenda is the albatross that has a stranglehold around the fiscal neck of the American people.'"

"Dad, you don't need to sugarcoat your feelings."

"Ha ha. It gets worse. Let me try to answer the second question about squashing individual freedoms.

"Internally, rigid organizational rules require conformance. Time in grade and not accomplishment is rewarded. Individualism is suppressed. Experimentation is absent. 'Don't rock the boat; just show up to get your check' becomes the prevailing philosophy."

"The bureaucracy absorbs people so they don't have to think. The Constitution did not foresee uncontrolled, sprawling federal government agencies answering to no one while costing untold moneys that rob the private sector of job creation initiatives. These days, a government employee's primary purpose in life is to keep the environment until personal retirement. Indeed, bureaucracy has its own inertia – it has to keep growing to make room for promotions so civil servants can supervise more people or dollars and attain higher GS levels."

"Bureaucracies create secondary welfare systems. The bureaucrat's retirements are rewards for time in grade while suppressing accomplishment and individual freedoms – all at the expense of taxpayers for generations to come. Many live for decades on the dole, often with multiple retirements; hence becoming 'double dippers.' If America knew the extent of this practice, a revolution would take place with a vigor that rivaled 1776! Congress itself is a mini welfare nation."

"Bureaucracies create obstacles, called 'rules,' that stifle and/ or eliminate private enterprise initiatives. They create paper requirements that enable their processing habits and authority but do not add value to the economy. There are thousands of examples

– the Environmental Protection Agency comes immediately to mind – but I have a dozen others in mind."

"Once employed by the federal or state bureaucracy, the employee learns the 'entitlement game' in order to work the system. This means more benefits and increased salary without substantive accomplishment. This can only be characterized as a social/economic disease for which the only cure is elimination of the position, indeed the entire organization. Again, the loser is the private citizen, particularly those working at minimum wage."

"Bureaucracies stifle the private sector via sinecure jealousy. The result is an implicit malaise around the D.C. Beltway. Loyal corporate employees start taking the federal holidays off because nobody is there to do business with, particularly during December, when 'govies' must take their annual leave or lose it."

"Government bureaucracies also must spend taxpayer money or risk losing it; specifically, receive the same or less appropriations next year, which would result in status quo instead of the ability to hire more workers to accelerate the bureaucrat's promotion. Again, promotion is rewarded by budget increase without additional accomplishment of goods and/or services, and the taxpayer pays the price."

"Bureaucracy also creates and shelters disguised unemployment because its agencies require a legion of rent-a-cops to protect their big, beautiful buildings from terrorist activities. The Ronald Reagan Building of the Department of Commerce is a perfect example. More than 200 rent-a-cops 'protect' it, but al-Qaida would never attack this building. Send the people home, close the department and lock the door."

"In this digital age, there are more than 4,000 offices of the Department of Agriculture. This is symptomatic of the expanse of federal agencies at the expense of the American taxpayer. The services are available online. Why do we need to pay for the salaries and benefits of people who work in offices that should be shut down?

"Erin, as you know, I could go on for hours – that's how big the problem is. But let me cut it short and simply say: Washington is the problem. Your generation must find a way to eliminate this disease which my generation created. After all, a disease may take your body, but D.C. takes your lifestyle. You live to support the bureaucrats. This isn't fair at any cost. You need to rally your peers to defeat this assault on individual freedom by the bureaucrats who exist only to protect their positions. You must approach this with the same urgency as Paul Revere's warning from the church tower."

We were quiet for a while.

"Dad, will you please stop looking for those Russian satellites in the star-filled sky and answer the third question about limiting the welfare state?"

"Sure will, as soon as I pour myself a tad more Canadian to help my speaking voice. I'll list a few, but when I run out of fingers, I'll shut up."

"First, we need to improve the economy so legions of private enterprise workers don't seek the shelter of the bureaucracy in Washington or at our state capitals."

"Next, we need to equalize the benefits associated with private and public sector employment. Today's total federal employment package is so much better than an equivalent position in industry, it's no wonder there are so many applicants for those jobs. For the same salary, the govie gets free health care, an 11-month work year, no required overtime and no real performance pressure."

"Dad, wait a minute. Federal employees sometimes work overtime."

"Yes, that's right – like congressional staffers preparing the budget or White House staffers writing a speech. But the operative word is 'sometimes.'"

"Agency heads also must be given real hire/fire power based upon annual performance and cost reduction goals. And an employee must create real cost savings in order to remain in his or her position."

"The government must eliminate time-in-grade as a promotion criteria between GS levels. Promotions must be based upon performance. Period."

"We must eliminate the government employee's retirement package. Like the rest of us, they too must live with Social Security as the only 'safety net.'"

"As an employer, the government must devise entrance qualifications commensurate with the private sector. Standard Form 171, the application for federal employment, must require additional qualifications for potential employees."

"The Senior Executive Service must be drastically reduced. It's top-heavy, bloated and a graveyard for innovation. The government salary schedule stops at GS-15."

"We must increase the federal income tax on government employees in order to compensate for the cost of the individual's position to the private sector economy."

"And we can't be afraid to close agencies. Lock the doors and sell the buildings. Agencies that remain will have both their mission and staff dramatically reduced; the norm will be one out of every two positions eliminated. This process will start in Washington, D.C., and over a four-year period – one presidential term – will be spread to remote offices across America."

"Wait a minute, Dad. You're talking about eliminating over a million jobs!"

"Yes, and tomorrow when we talk about debt reduction, another million are no longer needed in military uniform."

"Is America ready for such a second revolution?"

"Erin, when I lay out the debt situation, you'll see we have no choice. But – and this is a big but – Congress and the president must be of the same political persuasion. And they can't be aligned with the liberal party that started the Great Society in the first place. You see, Erin, as the economist Ludwig von Mises wrote in *The Freeman* in May 1953, 'there is no remedy for the inefficiency of public management' – well, no remedy short of major social change. The advocates of public spending must be stopped before another dollar is printed."

Chapter Four:
"THE NATIONAL DEBT"

"Dad, my boot is leaking."

"OK. Come ashore and we'll check it."

After rummaging around in the fishing kit, I found a couple inner tube patches. Just 10 minutes later, Erin, armed with a fly rod and smeared with anti-mosquito ointment, waded back into the stream to continue casting.

"If it's too small, we release it," I reminded her.

"Of course."

"Hey, Dad, I'm getting into pretty deep water here."

What a perfect moment to bring up today's topic, I thought.

"Deep water, you say? That's exactly what the U.S. economy is in. Our debt, disease number three, is no longer sustainable, much less defensible."

"Yes, I know. I've read some scary statistics. Do you think it's really that bad?"

"Well, Erin, you're the math whiz. Let me ask you a question: How many zeroes in $1 trillion?"

"Twelve."

"Right."

"Sooooo …"

"So, I just want to put our national debt into perspective."

"A trillion dollars is so much money, if you spent a dollar every second, it would take you 32,748 years to spend it. And our current national debt is approaching $16 trillion, or $137,000 per taxpayer. Maybe if I put it another way, it's easier to understand. The U.S. national debt on Jan. 1, 1791, was $75 million. Today, the U.S. national debt rises by that amount every hour."

"That's a powerful statistic. I knew it was bad, but not that bad!"

"Well, it's about to get personal."

"What do you mean?"

"It's a crisis of unsustainable proportion that must be dealt with by your generation. Since 1964 and the Great Society, two generations have not solved the problem. Each president has kicked the can down the road. Now the bill must be paid. But the federal government, which controls one-sixth of the economy, won't take the steps necessary to dismantle the welfare state. Indeed, there's even an arrogance in Washington that emboldens the administration to order private companies to provide employees with 'free' services such as medical coverage over and above a company's health plan, all at considerable expense. This is an assault on both free enterprise and the Constitution."

"In 1809, President Thomas Jefferson wrote a letter to his Secretary of the Treasury, Albert Gallatin, in which he described the national debt as a cesspool of patronage and corruption. He warned that the debt would commit the nation 'to the English career of debt, corruption and rottenness, closing with revolution.'

We moved downstream about 50 yards, where I untangled my line and prepared to cast.

"Dad, look! There's an eagle circling above."

No sooner were the words spoken than a magnificent raptor swooped down and snatched a fish from the very spot in the stream we had just left.

We can learn a lot from the bald eagle, I thought to myself. He was so fast, I probably wouldn't have had time to get a picture of him in action.

"Erin, that eagle is trying to tell us something."

"What?"

"I don't know. Maybe he wants me to expound upon the debt crisis so you'll be better able to explain it via social media when we return home."

"Did you know that the total debt added by the 43 U.S. presidents between 1789 and 2008 was $10.6 trillion?"

"No."

"And what's really scary is that the 44th president has added $6 trillion to the national debt in just three years!"

"Indeed, the current national debt is so large that the federal government now borrows about $4 billion per day. In fact, it has to borrow 43 cents of every dollar that it spends. That's four times the rate just 30 years ago. We can't even pay the interest, much less the principal. Indeed, according to the Cato Institute, a well-known Think Tank in Washington, America's debt is approaching the "Tipping Point" of 90% of the Gross Domestic Product (GDP). What this means is that a downturn in economic growth, war or even natural disaster could push the economy into a melt-down crisis."

"And, as you know, the federal government is operating without a credible budget that addresses the debt. Rather than propose spending cuts, the budget takes credit for prior spending cuts and proposes to replace some of those cuts with increased taxes. So you don't have to be a Nobel Prize-winning economist to understand that unsustainable government spending is pushing the nation ever closer to a crisis fueled by the debt. It's like pushing an eagle chick out of the nest."

"And it's up to my generation to fix this mess?"

"Oh, yes. It's your generation's job, all right. The next 15 years, perhaps just the next five years, will be critical for the U.S. and the world. And though I'm not an economist, common 'cents' shows how the national debt impacts every citizen. First, through higher taxes: To avoid going broke, the federal government will have no choice but to raise taxes or drastically reduce spending or both. If history is a guide, you'll be paying higher taxes for a long time. And guess what?"

"What?"

"According to the Heritage Foundation, a respected think tank, the percentage of people who do not pay federal income taxes, and who are not claimed as dependents by someone who does pay them, jumped from 14.8 percent in 1984 to 49.5 percent in 2009. This means 151.7 million Americans paid nothing in 2009."

"How is this possible?"

"Well, about 45 percent of U.S. households tell the IRS they are living on an income below the tax table threshold. They accomplish this by reducing their income in the 'taxable income' category, and they cut the remainder through qualified tax credits. The math is straightforward, and a sizeable number get a refund."

"So how will the government pay off the debt under these circumstances?"

"The simple answer is that it will have to cut spending by shrinking the welfare state and bringing the troops home."

"Of course, higher taxes are just one way debt affects our nation's citizens. The second major impact is reduced benefits and programs – everything from child care to Medicare to student financial aid."

"The third consequence is the eventual reluctance of investors and foreign governments to purchase Treasury bonds, thereby forcing interest rates to rise. All types of loans will cost more, further reducing economic growth."

"And, finally, as history has shown, when a government takes drastic steps to eliminate national debt, the currency is allowed to plummet in value so the debt is paid in cheaper dollars. High inflation usually results."

"Dad, suppose we manage to pay off the national debt? Then what?"

"Glad you asked. The debt would start accumulating all over again because the welfare state entitlement programs would still be growing faster than revenues come into the Treasury. And when debt grows faster than the Gross Domestic Product, the nation remains in an unsustainable fiscal trap, or cesspool, as Jefferson called it. So paying off the debt doesn't get the job done unless we also put an end to the U.S. welfare state."

"I hear what you're saying."

"Good. Well, we've got three fish in our basket. Let's call it a glorious day and head back to the lodge. I need to gather my thoughts for tomorrow, when I'll detail how we're going to solve this problem."

CHAPTER FIVE:

"FLIGHT PATH"

"Erin, this is our last day, so we need to make the most of it. After we finish breakfast, we'll check out of the lodge and catch the boat for Homer."

An hour later, we dropped our luggage off at the dockmaster's cabin in preparation for our seaplane flight later in the day.

"Where to first, Dad?"

"We're going to hike to the westernmost part of the town called Homer Spit. It's actually the most western tip of the American highway system."

"What's there?"

"An RV camp and some modest houses."

"And?"

"Have you ever heard of the Eagle Lady?"

"You're kidding, right?"

"No, I'm quite serious. A famous woman, Jean Keene, lived on the spit and fed eagles every winter for 30 years. People came from all over the world to see her and photograph the eagles. Keene was as tough as Alaska. In the 1950s she worked as a rodeo trick rider until she broke her leg in 80 places during a performance. She survived automobile accidents and breast cancer, earned a living as a truck driver and a pet groomer. When she began feeding eagles in 1977, she found herself at the center of a controversy. Some city folks thought Keene was helping the eagles consume too many fish."

"Eventually, the Homer City Council passed an ordinance banning the feeding of eagles and other birds, but exempted the Eagle Lady. She had a huge fan base, and she really helped put Homer on the map. She died at her home on January 13, 2009. A friend told the Homer News that, as her health declined, 'From her bed she could look right out the window and there was an eagle, almost like it was watching, guarding over her.'

"There are hundreds of eagles alive today because of this remarkable woman, Erin. That's why we're going where we're going."

Thirty minutes later, we arrived at a campground that jutted out into the incredible blue water of the Kachemak Bay. We took off our backpacks and put them on a picnic table. In silence, we walked along the shore in a reflective peace while scanning the horizon for a glimpse of America's symbol. Our little tribute to the eagle lady was heartfelt.

Erin broke the silence.

"I now understand something more about you, Dad, and why you were so keen to show me this beautiful place."

"I'm glad you appreciate it. This paradise has been a logical backdrop for the heavy conversations we've had over the past few days. I'm motivated because I don't want to lose our way of life to the three diseases attacking our republic."

"On day one, when you caught a fish, we talked about the deteriorating work ethic in our country. We talked about businesses with no customer loyalty and employees who never see the customer. We broached a tricky topic – the private sector fleeing to the public sector and exacerbating the welfare state. I asked: Why is there a generation that can't look you in the eye?"

"On day two we talked about the rise of the Great Society into an unsustainable welfare state crushing individual freedoms by destroying the economy. I explained that Washington is the problem."

"Yesterday we talked about the national debt and its potential to cause higher taxes, higher interest rates, and higher inflation but lower benefits. The debt is created and fed by the bureaucracy, which, by its nature, expands due to the organizational requirement to hire more people to ensure personal promotion – all at the expense of the citizens."

"What I hear you saying is that in order to avoid the fate of Rome, America needs a plan that simultaneously treats all three diseases."

"Yes … and sooner rather than later."

A few minutes later, it was time to move on.

"Let's head back to town, Erin. I want to show you the Alaska Islands and Ocean Visitor Center – it serves as a gateway to the Alaska Maritime Refuge Center, the largest seabird refuge in the world. You can bet we'll see Jonathan Livingston Seagull there … or at least one of his relatives. After all, this is the halibut fishing capital of the world."

Before long we were exploring the center, taking dozens of pictures and settling in for lunch under a clump of pines.

"This is quite a setting to talk about a social revolution, Dad, particularly one on this scale."

"You're right. In order to succeed in reversing the welfare state and eliminating the debt, a second American revolution is required. What's so remarkable about the first one is that it was successful. This Second Revolution must also succeed because in many ways the fate of the *global* economy is at stake. China owns so much of our debt; if we crash, it's very likely we'll start a global cascade of failed economies."

"Dad, let's walk back to the city center. I need an espresso to keep up with this dialog."

As we sat down at the café's outside table, a cruise liner gently docked nearby.

"I wonder if those tourists know about the eagles," I said.

"The odds of seeing one are very good – it's probably why many booked the trip. Now getting a good picture, that's another matter."

"That's for sure. May I pick up where we left off?"

"Certainly."

"We need three things for this revolution to succeed: an Action Plan, legions of informed citizens, and new federal policies.

"I bet I know what the animal symbol will be."

"Of course: the bald eagle. The plan starts with an informed online social media networks that unite liberty-minded citizens of all generations. Then this grassroots movement gains momentum in the media. People are hungry for a vision and leadership to implement it. The grassroots movement becomes a groundswell that gives ordinary citizens like you and me the courage to tell our elected officials – Republican, Democrat and Independent – to adopt the Bald Eagle Vision. If they don't, the next election cycle should send them home."

"How long do you think this revolution will take, Dad?"

"Probably five to six years. It'll take time because the current representatives and senators will fight to preserve the status quo. And, of course, our form of government needs a vote-getting consensus between the executive and legislative branches to effect major change, particularly change of this magnitude."

"That's true."

"The next component of the solution is policy. We must adopt national policies that make 'common cents.' Here's my short list:

- Reduce debt.
    - Amend the U.S. Constitution to require a balanced budget. The president must show <u>real</u> progress in every State of the Union address – no more reductions in the rate of cost growth; there must be absolute reductions.
    - Freeze the debt limit; no new money can be printed or borrowed
    - Return to the gold standard so the dollar remains the preferred exchange currency.
    - Collect unpaid taxes. The Internal Revenue Service estimates that Americans underpay taxes by $385 billion annually.
    - Research the impact of a flat tax for individuals and corporations.
    - Research the impact of a tax credit for individuals who prove annual savings.

- Overhaul the public education system and put the control back at the school district level where it belongs.

- Dismantle the welfare state several departments and agencies at a time.

- Bring the troops home. We can no longer afford to be the world's police force or nation builder. Besides, many of our technologies are a decade ahead of the rest of the world. This gives us time to get our priorities straight and fix the home front.

- Dramatically reduce the intelligence community.

- Reduce foreign aid by 80 percent.

- Raise the eligibility age for Social Security by two years.

- Develop economic stimulus industries (we'll call them ESIs – one more acronym won't hurt America). These are industries, like genetics and human flight, where low-cost foreign labor prevents profits in the United States.

"You see, Erin, unless we take all of the above steps, we're not breaking the work ethic/welfare state/debt stranglehold on our republic."

"Well, you know I'm your liberal daughter. You'll have to do some explaining to convince me to send the first text message endorsing this plan."

"I knew I would. But maybe logic will prevail.

"First, this revolution is more important than that critical day we put a man on the moon. I had tears in my eyes when Neil Armstrong stepped onto the surface of the moon back in July of 1969, and 2 billion people were glued to their televisions. It was awesome, but – and this is a big 'but' – the national economy and our way of life were not at stake then as they are now.

"Today, given the precarious state of national economies, we dare not precipitate a global depression. You can't imagine the suffering."

"True. So how do you turn the policy into a viable plan?"

I thought for a minute, aware that we only had a few hours before we'd have to catch our flight to Anchorage. This better be good.

"Not without you and the other millions of the 'Gifted Generation' who are paying off their college loans, trying to start a family in a miserable economy and have little or no savings for retirement. They may also be looking for a job or even living with their parents."

"We have to improve the situation."

"Yes, Erin, <u>we</u> have to do it – one email or text message at a time."

"So what's the plan?"

"Well, here goes. I'll go into more detail about the items I just listed.

"First, debt reduction. We need a constitutional amendment for a balanced budget. This puts the pressure on both the executive and legislative branches to prove absolute reductions, which initiates a whole series of actions that eliminate unnecessary expenditures in today's economy.

"Second, we freeze the debt limit. This forces the Federal Reserve to live within its means; it can't devalue our currency or lower interest rates any further.

"Third, overhaul the public education system. This means eliminating the Department of Education. It has no value for the student. The No Child Left Behind program is a disaster of government equality planning. What's more, the department hasn't increased teacher qualifications to meet the intellect of today's students. It supports the current teacher seniority ladder, which is defunct. It supports giving each student a second chance at grades. Life is not like that, so why should the education system encourage this?"

"Fourth, dismantle the welfare state. If we are serious about cutting government, we need to ax entire missions, departments and programs. John Stossel of Fox News has done an excellent job of highlighting the need to eliminate entire federal government departments in order to balance the budget. He points out how the Canadian government works to balance its budget and reverse the Big Government syndrome of waste, fraud and abuse."

"Dad, I need to interrupt you. Is there any precedent for trying to eliminate entire federal departments?"

"Well, it isn't pretty. Indeed, they have all survived in spite of their incompetence and unnecessary drain on the Treasury. This goes back to 1980, when President Ronald Reagan campaigned to eliminate the Education and Energy Departments. Too bad he failed for reasons too numerous for our short discussion."

"OK. I understand. What standards would we use to eradicate a government entity?"

"Good question. We could start with these criteria:

- It's strictly an entitlement agency created by the Great Society.

- It has a huge budget with suspect value added to the economy.

- The service belongs at the state level.

- It's a duplicate agency.

- The agency exists because of the terrorist threat.

- The service should be privatized.

- The agency exists to provide foreign aid.

- It only exists for political pork barrel reasons."

"Those seem reasonable."

"Erin, did you know that an eagle can see moving prey from a thousand feet? It can even see fish under the water. It surveys an area of three square miles from its nest."

"What's your point?"

"That you don't have to be an eagle eye to see the reality that if every other federal employee were given a pink slip, service would not deteriorate. Therefore, the organizations that are not eliminated would be cut in half, at least, on a case-by-case basis."

"What's your shortlist of those that should be padlocked?"

"The Department of Agriculture, though some food programs would remain; the Department of Housing and Urban Development; the Department of Labor, except for unemployment benefits; the Department of Commerce, except for weather reporting services; and the Departments of Education and Interior. Several services like the

U.S. Postal Service and Transportation Security Administration would be privatized, but the security employees at airports would be cut by 90 percent. This is disguised unemployment in areas where this is no credible threat."

"And the military?"

"The troops come home and the defense budget is cut by two-thirds or almost $500 billion. The remaining budget would still be twice that of China's defense expenditures. We must stop being the shadow defense department for dozens of countries. Our current arsenal is state-of-the-art, so no new planes, ships or tanks would be built for five years. The Constitution calls for the protection of our citizens, not policing the globe or nation building."

"And foreign aid?"

"It's cut by 80 percent until the budget is balanced. After that, we can provide humanitarian assistance one nation at a time."

"What else?"

"There are 19 entities in America's intelligence community. I believe we should only have six: one each for the Army, Navy, Air Force, and the Central Intelligence Agency, National Reconnaissance Office and National Security Agency. However, at all of these every other car in the parking lot would disappear."

"Dad, what's your plan for dismantling these agencies?"

"Well, it's very complicated. How about we save the details for another trip?"

"Fair enough. But you must have some general ideas."

"I do indeed. Let's consider this one: Have you ever heard of the Base Realignment and Closure process, or BRAC?"

"Yes. It's an attempt by the Department of Defense to trim its infrastructure by consolidating locations."

"Right. But there's a tragic flaw."

"What's that?"

"It doesn't work. You see, a military base is closed. Some senior civil servants retire and some move to a new location. However, at the new location are many new, huge buildings."

"So?"

"These new buildings must be filled with people to justify their construction. It's the Law of Bureaucracy to fill these new spaces. So in effect it's a shell game that doesn't save the taxpayer a dime. However, there *is* something valuable that has resulted from this process: checklists of steps, processes and documents that must be followed and/or completed to ensure a successful base closure.

"And one of the bases, maybe one near the nation's capital, could house a command post for what I call the Civilian Closure Corps (CCC)."

"You see, I believe any country that can do the meticulous planning necessary to build and destroy intercontinental ballistic missiles can create closure teams responsible for padlocking government agencies. And, of course, their existence would only be temporary – as long as it takes to close an agency, process its people, and sell or retrofit the buildings for private sector use."

"Why use a military base for this activity?"

"My guess is that these closure teams would be feared almost as much as the Tax Man. They would require the isolation and protection that a military base would offer."

"And where do you get the recruits for this venture?"

"Just like the whiz kids under President Johnson who crafted the Great Society, civil servants and retired military personnel would clamor to be on these teams because they would be the last entities to be eliminated. I also believe that congressional staffers would be some of the first to sign up for these teams with a Peace Corps-like fervor."

"Why?"

"Because congressional budgets will be slashed, the staff offices will be only as large as necessary to support the passage of bills – they'll no longer serve as campaign machines to keep the representative or senator in office. Hence, these citizens can serve the nation in another capacity by joining the CCC."

"It's kind of ironic, really."

"What do you mean?"

"The staffers will be participating in an activity which their former bosses would never dream of – namely, closing federal agencies and departments. And the CCC would also attract returning veterans who already believe in national service, but this time would be saving the nation from itself instead of an elusive terrorist organization."

"How about Medicare or Medicaid? What happens to them?"

"We would have to increase the deductibles and premiums while working vigilantly to eliminate fraudulent claims. Also, we have the Statue of Liberty on one coast, the Golden Gate Bridge on the other welcoming people to our shores, yet we're building a fence along our southern border. This is nonsense. Bring the unmanned aircraft home – they'll find the smugglers."

"Dad, this is really serious. I can imagine people across the country would demonstrate because of these cuts."

"I can, too. The elected officials will have to go public as often as necessary to remind the nation that the alternative to a failed economy is unacceptable, indeed, un-American."

"All these cuts would leave a lot of people out of work."

"That brings me to the fifth major feature of the plan: job creation in the private sector. It's the private sector's inventors and entrepreneurs who create products and services that never occur to federal bureaucrats, primarily because they are not motivated by profit."

"What's needed is investment in industries where America has a technological advantage and can create a product that could only be manufactured overseas by lower cost labor once we perfect it, protect it and gain long-term royalties. These products might include next generation internal combustion engines; lightweight batteries; mobile internet applications; handheld, miniaturized medical diagnostic devices; genetics for increased bounty and longevity of foodstuffs; new composite materials, perhaps strengthened by lumber resins; and human flight."

"Human flight?"

"Just what I said. America gave the world the airplane, computer, electricity, radio, television, telephone and the internet. We can do human flight in the next decade. Don't spend federal money on space exploration; leave that to industry.

"Think about it. For 2,000 years humans have wanted to be like the eagle. We've got hot air balloons, parasails, gliders, hang gliders, winged suits and even the Swiss Rocketman, Ives Rossy. They all have one thing in common: overcoming gravity for individual freedom."

"Wouldn't you like to sit in a little capsule while flying past a traffic jam?"

"Sure, but you can't neutralize gravity."

"That's right. You would have to violate the Law of Conservation of Energy or …"

"Or what?"

"Find a way to combine a lightweight power source with a lightweight propulsion unit and reliable flight control surfaces."

"Dad, I think this is a flight of fancy. Flying cars are a long way off."

"That may be, but the nation needs a new industry to create jobs like the Space Race."

"That took 10 years."

"Yes, and a lot of spin-off industries employed nearly 1 million people over that period."

"Well, maybe a national competition could lead to a feasible solution."

"Speaking of flight, let's head down to the marina. It's about time to catch our plane."

Chapter Six:
"LIFT-OFF"

We retrieved our luggage and sat on a bench at the end of the pier. I zipped up my windbreaker and took in the sights and sounds.

"Erin, look at that glow of the setting sun on the western range."

"Awesome."

"You know, America was so lucky to purchase Alaska from Russia. We got timber, fish, gold, oil and so much beauty. Photographs don't do it justice. I'm glad I got to discover this great state with you. Thanks for accepting my invitation to do this. And thanks for letting me talk your ear off!"

"Well, Dad, I have to say I didn't know what I was getting into at first, but it's been great. I learned a lot about you. And I learned a lot about our country's challenges. Politically, I came here a staunch liberal. Now I'm not so sure. Your Bald Eagle Vision concept may just have wings."

"You know, the only true joy in life comes from helping others. But helping a nation successfully revolt – that's a whole new world."

A few minutes later, the seaplane approached.

"You know, Dad, I get it now. You want to turn the Great Society into the Grateful Society where all citizens appreciate a sound economy based upon compassion and innovation that leads the world to a more prosperous future."

"Erin, I couldn't have said it better myself."

We then boarded the floating bird, buckled our seatbelts and followed the pilot's instructions. I stared out the window across the bay. I could see the lodge and the campfire site. Just then a loud screeching sound came out of nowhere. It was a bald eagle skimming low across the water at breakneck speed, screeching as if to say, "Goodbye and good luck!"

The engine revved up and we gained enough speed for a take-off. As the water dripped from the pontoons and we headed east over the tree line, I tapped my daughter on the shoulder and said, "You may be the next Paul Revere."

She knew what I meant.

About the Author

Jason O'Neil, a spacecraft and telecommunications marketing executive for over 35 years, has travelled around the world working with national governments to implement advanced communications systems. He is credited with the lead role in the sale and launch of over 30 communications satellites. As such, he understands how governments and bureaucracies work or don't work. As a Son of the American Revolution, Marine officer in Vietnam and Knight of Malta for humanitarian deeds, Mr. O'Neil has a seasoned view of complex government and private organizations and their role to serve or hinder a national economy. Most recently, he has been a student of the relationship between government debts and the erosion of personal freedoms. He lives in the Washington DC area.

BALD EAGLE IMAGES

The photographs in this book are copyrighted
by the following photographers:

Cary Anderson

Grant Collier

Travis Novitsky

Dave Levandusky

Matt Shetzer

Many of the photographs were taken on location in
Alaska, often at considerable personal effort.

The author wishes to recognize these professionals for their ability
to so aptly capture the essence and spirit of our national symbol.